The Earth and Me

MIKE ARTELL AND PAM SCHILLER

GoodYear Books

An Imprint of ScottForesman
A Division of HarperCollinsPublishers

GoodYearBooks

are available for most basic curriculum subjects plus many enrichment areas. For more GoodYearBooks, contact your local bookseller or educational dealer. For a complete catalog with information about other GoodYearBooks, please write:

GoodYearBooks

ScottForesman
1900 East Lake Avenue
Glenview, IL 60025

Illustration: Mike Artell
Design: Lynne Grenier Design

The Earth and Me

Table of Contents

Introduction 1

Using this Book 2

Home-School Connections 3

Tips for Making Flannel Board Pieces...5

1. The Sun

Things to Think About..12

Things to Talk About 13

Things We Can Do 14

    Plant Comparison 14

    Shadows 14

      Sun Patterns 14

       Sun Dials 16

        Fun in the Sun..17

        Rainbows 17

      Fast and Fun 18

    Family Notes 19

      Bibliography 20

2. Water

Things to Think About 26

Things to Talk About 27

Things We Can Do 28

    Water Colors...28

    Growing Things...29

    Finger Gelatin 29

    Sidewalk Art 30

    Plant Drinks 30

    Drop Count 31

    Funnel Fun 32

    Bathe the Baby 32

Fast and Fun 33

Family Notes 34

Bilbliography 35

3. Air

Things to Think About 44

Things to Talk About 45

Things We Can Do 46

    Straw Blowing...46

    Ping Pong Ball Race 47

    Air Tent 47

    Meringue 49

Paper Planes 49

Good Smells 50

Fast and Fun 51

Family Notes...52

Bibliography 53

4. Soil

Things to Think About 60

Things to Talk About 61

Things We Can Do 62

    Clay Sculptures 62

    Sand Painting 63

    Soil Words..63

    Micro Life 64

    Rich Dirt/Poor Dirt 65

    Vegetable Classification...66

    Making Sand...66

    Making Mud 67

Fast and Fun 68

Family Notes 69

Bibliography 70

5. Trees and Plants

Things to Think About 78

Things to Talk About 79

Things We Can Do 81

    Autumn Leaves 81

    Leaf Classification..82

    Windowsill Vegetable Plants..82

    Vegetable Soup...83

    Tree Trunk Rubbings 83

    Leaf Rubbings 84

    Leaf Bracelets 84

Fast and Fun 85

Family Notes 86

Bibliography 87

6. Endangered Species

Things to Think About 94

Things to Talk About 95

Things We Can Do 96

    Animal Friends 96

    Animal Sort 97

    Zoo Homes 97

    Advocate Posters 98

    Animal Homes 99

    Animal Collage 99

Fast and Fun 100

Family Notes 100

Bibliography 101

7. Litter

Things to Think About 112

Things to Talk About 113

Things We Can Do 114

    Trash to Treasure 114

    Litter Toss 114

    Litter Busters 115

    Litter Detectives 116

        Fast and Fun 117

        Family Notes 117

        Bibliography 118

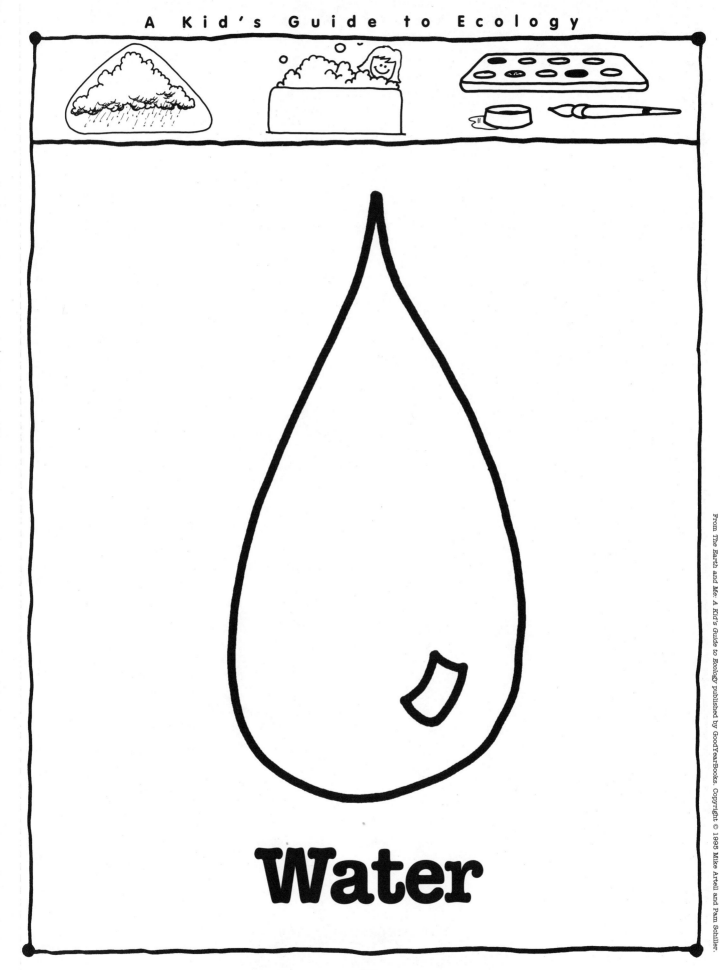

Water

From *The Earth and Me: A Kid's Guide to Ecology* published by GoodYearBooks. Copyright © 1995 Mike Artell and Pam Schiller.

Art Patterns

Water

Water

The Water

Hi, I'm a drop of water.

By myself, I'm not very strong, but when I get together with lots of my friends, you'd be surprised what we can do.

When we fall from a cloud, my friends and I make rain. Soft summer rain that waters the grass and the flowers, and heavy, noisy thunderstorms that wash away dirt and stones.

We make streams and rivers and ponds and lakes. Even oceans!

Clean, fresh water. It's great to drink, and it's just right to swim in. It's perfect for washing clothes and for washing people. Everything that lives needs water . . . plants, animals and people.

Clean, fresh water.

Very Funny Stuff

Hi again!

You may not know it, but water can be very funny.

That's right!

Most of the time, water just sits around in a little puddle, but when water gets hot or cold, some funny things happen.

When water gets cold enough, it turns to ice. Brrrr!

That's when it gets cold and hard.

When lots of water turns to ice, it can make icebergs and glaciers.

But . . . when water gets hot, something very different happens.

First it starts to bubble, then it turns to steam and floats off into the air.

When water gets this hot it is very dangerous, but it can also be a big help.

If water is hot enough, it can cook food and run machines to help us do work.

A long time ago, people even had cars that used hot water to move them.

Water can be wet and drippy or cold and hard or hot and steamy.

Water can be very funny stuff.

Water

Things to think about

1. Water is precious. It is powerful. It is magic.

2. Most of the water we drink comes from rivers, lakes and streams.

3. Water is vital to the health of plants, animals and humans.

4. Water from rivers, lakes and streams becomes toxic (poisonous) if people dump toxic or poisonous trash underground.

5. Rain does not fall evenly over the earth. Droughts occur in many parts of the world and can mean death, disease and disaster.

6. Water can be conserved by

   - Turning off the faucet when brushing your teeth.
   - Taking 3-minute showers.
   - Watching for leaky faucets. Tell an adult.
   - Keeping water in the refrigerator for drinking instead of running the faucet until the water gets cold.

7. Many people earn their living from the earth's water (fishing, shelling, etc.)

From *The Earth and Me: A Kid's Guide to Ecology* published by GoodYearBooks. Copyright © 1995 Mike Artell and Pam Schiller.

Water

Things to talk about

1. Name all the ways that we use water (brushing our teeth, cooking, bathing, cleaning paint brushes, etc.).

2. How many ways can you think of to help save water (turning off the water when we brush our teeth, using less water when we bathe, using rain water for watering plants)?

3. The water we use in our schools and houses comes in and goes out through pipes. The pipes from lots of schools and houses are connected. Where do you think the water goes when it leaves your school or house?

From *The Earth and Me: A Kid's Guide to Ecology* published by GoodYearBooks. Copyright © 1995 Mike Artell and Pam Schiller.

Water

Things We Can Do

Water Colors • Materials: Watercolors, brushes, paper

Procedure:

1. Encourage the children to paint with water-colors without the use of water.
2. Ask the children why the paints don't work.
3. Allow the children to create pictures using watercolors with water.

Concept: Water is a substance that we frequently use to enhance other substances.

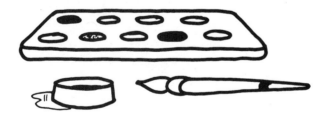

Fast and Fun

- Make and fly paper airplanes.
- Make paper pinwheels.
- Study windmills.
- Fly a kite.
- Make bathtub sailboats with bars of ivory soap, toothpicks and paper sails.
- Blow bubbles with dishwashing liquid.
- Recite "Twinkle, twinkle, little star." Explain that dust in the air makes stars appear to twinkle.

Air

From *The Earth and Me: A Kid's Guide to Ecology* published by GoodYearBooks. Copyright © 1995 Mike Artell and Pam Schiller.

Family Notes

Air • Things to do at home:

- Fly a kite. Help children determine the effects of air on the kite's movement.
- Predict the amount of wind blowing outside by looking through a window to observe the movement of leaves or the amount of clothing people are wearing.
- Make meringue at home (use recipe from school activity)
- Use the weather chart symbols to report wind conditions each day (windy, calm, etc.)

Related Bibilography

Ets, Mary. *Gilberto and the Wind*. Viking 1963. Gilberto learns about all the things the wind can do.

Keats, Ezra Jack. *Whistle for Willie*. Viking 1964. Peter wants to whistle so he can call his dog.

LaFontaine. *The North Wind and the Sun*. Oxford 1987. Two weather giants try to make a man take off his coat.

Lambert, David. *The Work of the Wind*. Bookwright 1989. An excellent reference book for facts about the wind.

Meyer, Mercer. *Bubble, Bubble*. Publishing Group West, 1992. A little boy creates all kinds of fantastic animals with his magic bubble maker.

Schmid, Eleonore. *The Air Around Us*. North-South Books, 1992. A simple explanation of the role air plays in weather and in sustaining life on earth. Beautiful illustrations support the text.

Air

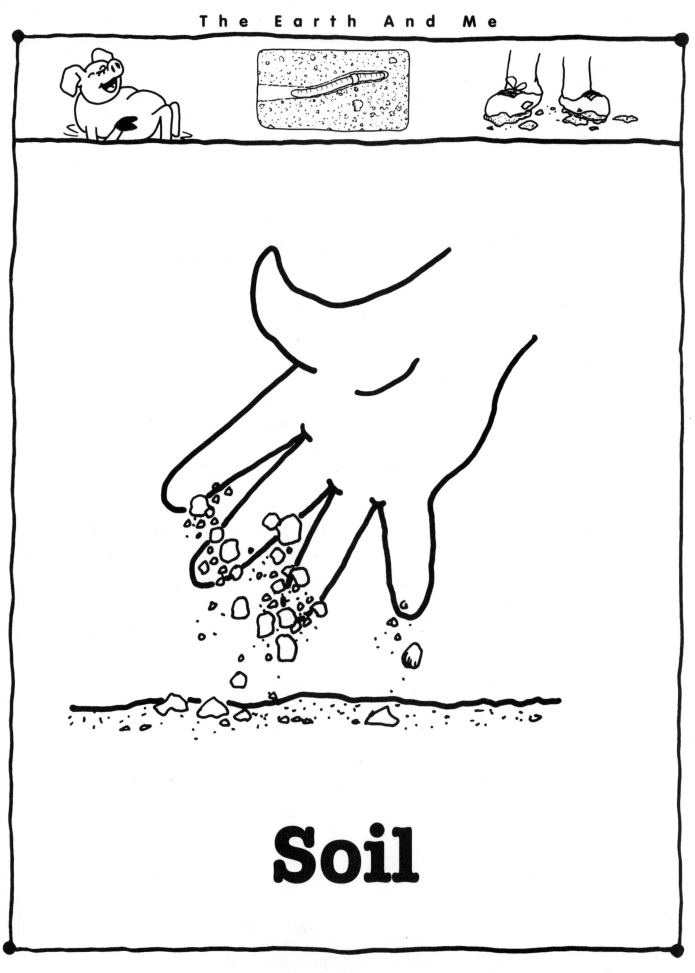

Soil

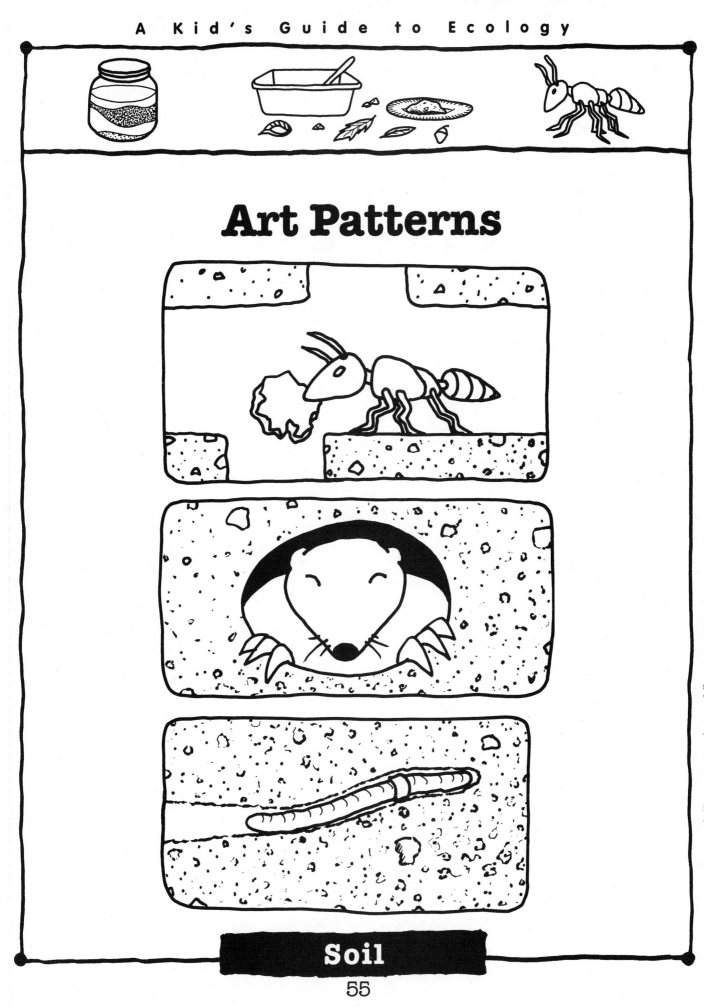

Art Patterns

Soil

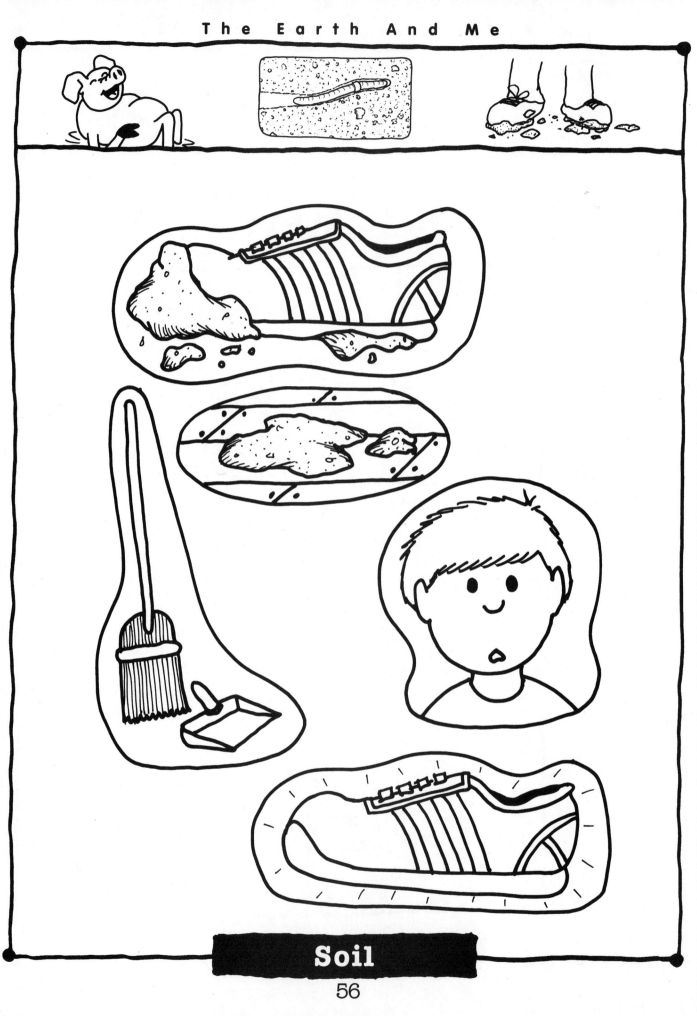

Soil

California Condor, Humpback Whale

California Condor, Humpback Whale
big strong wings and big strong tail,

are you safe in your nest
are you safe in the sea?

The earth is big enough
for you and me.

Endangered Species

See Ya' Later Alligator!

Not long ago in the swamp they say, the green alligator almost faded away.

People used to hunt them and take their skin, and the 'gator population was gettin' mighty thin.

Then the people stopped one day and they said, "Just a minute. This swamp had lots of 'gators, now there aren't many in it. Maybe if we wait, the old 'gators will return." So they climbed out of the swamp and they hid behind a fern.

It took a while to happen, but the 'gators did come back
with their big white teeth and their big bumpy backs,
You have to care for things if you want to see them later
like the ferns and the swamp and the green alligator.

Author's note: The alligator was once endangered, but now scientists estimate that there are nearly one million alligators in the United States. Source: ZooBooks, Wildlife Education Ltd.

Endangered Species

Who's in the Zoo?

Sometimes, animals live in zoos so people can study them. The people study what the animals eat and how they take care of their babies and lots of other things. They try to learn as much as they can about the animals. Some people even go to school to be doctors for animals. These people are called veterinarians.

The place where an animal lives is called its habitat. Some animals don't have as much habitat as they used to. When this happens, animals may have trouble finding food and shelter. Sometimes, zoos can help. Zoos try to build habitats for animals that are a lot like the animals' natural homes. The people in the zoos feed the animals and take care of them when they get sick.

It would be wonderful if all the animals had as much room as they wanted for their habitats. But there are lots of animals and lots of people and we all have to share the earth.

Since we have to share the earth with each other, it's good that people are trying to learn as much as they can about helping animals.

From *The Earth and Me: A Kid's Guide to Ecology* published by GoodYearBooks. Copyright © 1995 Mike Artell and Pam Schiller.

Endangered Species

Things to think about

1. People and animals both have to share the earth.

2. There are some animals, like dinosaurs, that are not around anymore. Sometimes human's progress caused this, other times they did not.

3. Once a species of animal is gone, it cannot return.

Endangered Species

Things to talk about

1. Have you ever seen an animal in a zoo that was an endangered species? (Siberian tiger, mountain gorilla, African elephant, Galapagos tortoise, Indian python). Tell about it.

2. Native americans used the bison as a source of food, clothing and tools. What other kinds of animal furs and skins have people worn? (rabbit, beaver, bear, mink, fox, leopard, alligator, snake)

3. What kinds of animal furs and skins to people still wear today? (rabbit, beaver, mink, fox, snake. Don't forget to include cow leather!)

4. Why is it against the law to wear the furs and skins of endangered animals?

5. Discuss success stories. Examples: Bison, Alligator, Eagle.

From *The Earth and Me: A Kid's Guide to Ecology* published by GoodYearBooks. Copyright © 1995 Mike Artell and Pam Schiller.

Endangered Species

Things We Can Do

Art

Animal Friends • Materials: Drawing paper, crayons

Procedure:

1. Have the children draw pictures of animals and humans sharing the earth.
2. Encourage children to describe their art to their classmates.

Concept: Animals and humans can live cooperatively.

Endangered Species

From *The Earth and Me: A Kid's Guide to Ecology* published by GoodYearBooks. Copyright © 1995 Mike Artell and Pam Schiller.

Science

Animal Sort • Materials: Pictures of animals, endangered and not endangered.

Procedure:
1. Talk about each animal in the pictures. Discuss those that are endangered and describe what caused them to be on this list.
2. Encourage children to classify the animals' pictures into endangered and not endangered.

Concept: Some animals are in danger of extinction.

Gross Motor

Zoo Homes • Materials: Blocks, plastic animals, construction paper, small cardboard boxes

Procedure:
1. Encourage the children to build a zoo to house the plastic animals.
2. Discuss the various needs of each animal and provide props for children to create adequate homes for the animals.

Endangered Species

From *The Earth and Me: A Kid's Guide to Ecology* published by GoodYearBooks. Copyright © 1995 Mike Artell and Pam Schiller.

Art

Rhythm Pictures • Materials: Tape recorder, tape, drawing paper, crayons

Procedure:

1. Have children draw pictures or just move their crayon across their paper while listening to music of different tempos.
2. Does faster music make us work faster?

Concept: Music has a beat that people often internalize.

Math

Counting Bells • Materials: Felt, velcro, glue, bells

Procedure:

1. Make five 4 in. x 4 in. bags from felt by gluing 3 sides of two 4 in. x 4 in. squares of felt together and by using a small piece of velcro as a fastener for the fourth side of the square.
2. Have children put 1 bell in the first bag, 2 in the second, 3 in the third, etc.
3. Ask the children to shake each bag. Can they

Noise

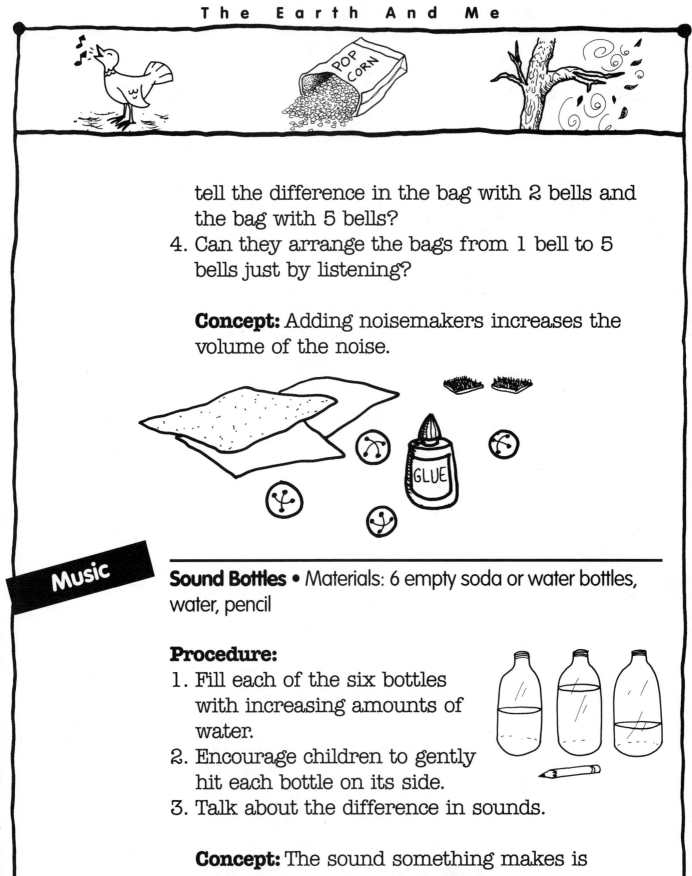

tell the difference in the bag with 2 bells and the bag with 5 bells?

4. Can they arrange the bags from 1 bell to 5 bells just by listening?

Concept: Adding noisemakers increases the volume of the noise.

From *The Earth and Me: A Kid's Guide to Ecology* published by GoodYearBooks. Copyright © 1995 Mike Artell and Pam Schiller.

Music

Sound Bottles • Materials: 6 empty soda or water bottles, water, pencil

Procedure:

1. Fill each of the six bottles with increasing amounts of water.
2. Encourage children to gently hit each bottle on its side.
3. Talk about the difference in sounds.

Concept: The sound something makes is related to its size and shape.

Noise

Discovery Center

Sound Vibrations • Materials: None

Procedure:

1. Have children place their hands on their throats.
2. Tell them to whisper their name. Tell them to say their names out loud.
3. What makes the difference in the sounds?

Concept: The vibration of our vocal cords creates sound.

Noise

From *The Earth and Me: A Kid's Guide to Ecology* published by GoodYearBooks. Copyright © 1995 Mike Artell and Pam Schiller.

Fast and Fun

- Have children put their ears on the table and tap their fingernails on the table at the same time. What happens to the sound of the tapping?
- Have someone demonstrate a dog whistle.
- Make paper cup telephones.
- Learn some simple sign language (Some people don't hear sounds).
- Make shoe box/tissue box and rubber band guitars.
- Place 6 inches of a ruler on a table and 6 inches hanging off the table. Hold down the part of the ruler on the table so it lies flat. Pluck the part hanging off the table and make it vibrate. Now move more of the ruler onto the table, pluck it again and listen for the higher tone. Move the ruler back and forth, experiment. Try to play "Mary Had a Little Lamb."
- Make megaphones out of construction paper. Megaphones concentrate sounds and make them louder. Discuss.
- Talk about sounds that tell us something. Horns on cars and trucks are warnings, the ringer on a telephone or a door bell tells us

Noise

someone is calling for us, video games make different sounds when you win and lose, cars make different sounds when they're running well and when they're not, tea kettles whistle to tell us water is boiling, smoke alarms go off when there is smoke in the room, animals growl when they are angry or scared.

- Make various "noisemakers" with dry beans in containers, etc.

- Shhhhhhh. Have a quiet 15 seconds where children are paying close attention to every single sound they hear both in the classroom and outside. When the 15 seconds are up, list the sounds on the board.

- Draw (or cut from a magazine) pictures of noisy places and quiet places, noisy animals and quiet animals, noisy things and quiet things.

- Blow up a balloon and pop it with a pin. Discuss all the sounds that went into this activity. (Includes removing balloon from the bag it came in, filling the balloon with air, tying a knot in the balloon and popping it)

- Pick something that's noisy and discuss how to make it quieter. Answers can be crazy, funny or practical.

From *The Earth and Me: A Kid's Guide to Ecology* published by GoodYearBooks. Copyright © 1995 Mike Artell and Pam Schiller.

Noise

Family Notes

Topic: Noise Pollution • Things to do at home:

- Discuss the ways that each family member wakes up each morning (alarm clock, radio, someone's call, etc.) What would it be like to wake up to a lawn mower or someone beating on pots and pans?

- Try having a quiet hour each evening . . . no television, no talking, no disturbances. Let each family member report on what they did with their quiet time.

- Talk about respecting other people's quiet space, not playing the stereo or television too loudly.

- Check out the book **LoudMouse** by Richard Wilbur from the library and read it with your child.